My Daily Living Skills Log

A monthly skill log

Based on the Core 6 books

from My Skills Books

My Skills Books | myskillsbooks.com

Copyright © 2025 by My Skills Books

Published by My Skills Books

All rights reserved. No part of this publication may be reproduced, distributed, or transmitted in any form or by any means, including photocopying, recording, or other electronic or mechanical methods, without the prior written permission of the publisher, except in the case of brief quotations embodied in critical reviews and certain other noncommercial uses permitted by copyright law.

First Printing, 2025.

ISBN: 978-1-951573-57-7

www.myskillsbooks.com

Table of Contents

	I Can Use The Bathroom	4-34
	I Can Wash My Hands	35-65
	I Can Brush My Teeth	66-96
	I Can Wash My Face	97-127
	I Can Take A Shower	128-158
	I Can Take A Bath	159-199

I Can Use The Bathroom

Skill Progress Log

Pull down underwear and bottoms	Y	N
Sit on toilet seat	Y	N
Pee or poop in toilet	Y	N
Get tissue	Y	N
Wipe self with tissue	Y	N
Put tissue in toilet	Y	N
Pull up underwear and bottoms	Y	N
Flush the toilet	Y	N
Go to sink and turn on faucet	Y	N
Lather soap in hands for 20 sec.	Y	N
Rinse hands with water	Y	N
Turn off sink faucet	Y	N
Dry hands	Y	N

Directions: Mark Y if the skill is performed without assistance and N if the skill required assistance to be completed.

Date: / /   Score:

I Can Use The Bathroom

Skill Progress Log

Pull down underwear and bottoms	Y	N
Sit on toilet seat	Y	N
Pee or poop in toilet	Y	N
Get tissue	Y	N
Wipe self with tissue	Y	N
Put tissue in toilet	Y	N
Pull up underwear and bottoms	Y	N
Flush the toilet	Y	N
Go to sink and turn on faucet	Y	N
Lather soap in hands for 20 sec.	Y	N
Rinse hands with water	Y	N
Turn off sink faucet	Y	N
Dry hands	Y	N

Directions: Mark Y if the skill is performed without assistance and N if the skill required assistance to be completed.

Date: /   /   Score:

I Can Use The Bathroom

Skill Progress Log

Pull down underwear and bottoms	Y	N
Sit on toilet seat	Y	N
Pee or poop in toilet	Y	N
Get tissue	Y	N
Wipe self with tissue	Y	N
Put tissue in toilet	Y	N
Pull up underwear and bottoms	Y	N
Flush the toilet	Y	N
Go to sink and turn on faucet	Y	N
Lather soap in hands for 20 sec.	Y	N
Rinse hands with water	Y	N
Turn off sink faucet	Y	N
Dry hands	Y	N

Directions: Mark Y if the skill is performed without assistance and N if the skill required assistance to be completed.

Date: / /   Score:

I Can Use The Bathroom

Skill Progress Log

Pull down underwear and bottoms	Y	N
Sit on toilet seat	Y	N
Pee or poop in toilet	Y	N
Get tissue	Y	N
Wipe self with tissue	Y	N
Put tissue in toilet	Y	N
Pull up underwear and bottoms	Y	N
Flush the toilet	Y	N
Go to sink and turn on faucet	Y	N
Lather soap in hands for 20 sec.	Y	N
Rinse hands with water	Y	N
Turn off sink faucet	Y	N
Dry hands	Y	N

Directions: Mark Y if the skill is performed without assistance and N if the skill required assistance to be completed.

Date: / /   Score:

I Can Use The Bathroom

Skill Progress Log

Pull down underwear and bottoms	Y	N
Sit on toilet seat	Y	N
Pee or poop in toilet	Y	N
Get tissue	Y	N
Wipe self with tissue	Y	N
Put tissue in toilet	Y	N
Pull up underwear and bottoms	Y	N
Flush the toilet	Y	N
Go to sink and turn on faucet	Y	N
Lather soap in hands for 20 sec.	Y	N
Rinse hands with water	Y	N
Turn off sink faucet	Y	N
Dry hands	Y	N

Directions: Mark Y if the skill is performed without assistance and N if the skill required assistance to be completed.

Date: /   /   Score:

I Can Use The Bathroom

Skill Progress Log

Pull down underwear and bottoms	Y	N
Sit on toilet seat	Y	N
Pee or poop in toilet	Y	N
Get tissue	Y	N
Wipe self with tissue	Y	N
Put tissue in toilet	Y	N
Pull up underwear and bottoms	Y	N
Flush the toilet	Y	N
Go to sink and turn on faucet	Y	N
Lather soap in hands for 20 sec.	Y	N
Rinse hands with water	Y	N
Turn off sink faucet	Y	N
Dry hands	Y	N

Directions: Mark Y if the skill is performed without assistance and N if the skill required assistance to be completed.

Date: /   /   Score:

I Can Use The Bathroom

Skill Progress Log

Pull down underwear and bottoms	Y	N
Sit on toilet seat	Y	N
Pee or poop in toilet	Y	N
Get tissue	Y	N
Wipe self with tissue	Y	N
Put tissue in toilet	Y	N
Pull up underwear and bottoms	Y	N
Flush the toilet	Y	N
Go to sink and turn on faucet	Y	N
Lather soap in hands for 20 sec.	Y	N
Rinse hands with water	Y	N
Turn off sink faucet	Y	N
Dry hands	Y	N

Directions: Mark Y if the skill is performed without assistance and N if the skill required assistance to be completed.

Date: / /   Score:

I Can Use The Bathroom

Skill Progress Log

Pull down underwear and bottoms	Y	N
Sit on toilet seat	Y	N
Pee or poop in toilet	Y	N
Get tissue	Y	N
Wipe self with tissue	Y	N
Put tissue in toilet	Y	N
Pull up underwear and bottoms	Y	N
Flush the toilet	Y	N
Go to sink and turn on faucet	Y	N
Lather soap in hands for 20 sec.	Y	N
Rinse hands with water	Y	N
Turn off sink faucet	Y	N
Dry hands	Y	N

Directions: Mark Y if the skill is performed without assistance and N if the skill required assistance to be completed.

Date: / /   Score:

I Can Use The Bathroom

Skill Progress Log

Pull down underwear and bottoms	Y	N
Sit on toilet seat	Y	N
Pee or poop in toilet	Y	N
Get tissue	Y	N
Wipe self with tissue	Y	N
Put tissue in toilet	Y	N
Pull up underwear and bottoms	Y	N
Flush the toilet	Y	N
Go to sink and turn on faucet	Y	N
Lather soap in hands for 20 sec.	Y	N
Rinse hands with water	Y	N
Turn off sink faucet	Y	N
Dry hands	Y	N

Directions: Mark Y if the skill is performed without assistance and N if the skill required assistance to be completed.

Date: /   /   Score:

I Can Use The Bathroom

Skill Progress Log

Pull down underwear and bottoms	Y	N
Sit on toilet seat	Y	N
Pee or poop in toilet	Y	N
Get tissue	Y	N
Wipe self with tissue	Y	N
Put tissue in toilet	Y	N
Pull up underwear and bottoms	Y	N
Flush the toilet	Y	N
Go to sink and turn on faucet	Y	N
Lather soap in hands for 20 sec.	Y	N
Rinse hands with water	Y	N
Turn off sink faucet	Y	N
Dry hands	Y	N

Directions: Mark Y if the skill is performed without assistance and N if the skill required assistance to be completed.

Date: / /   Score:

I Can Use The Bathroom

Skill Progress Log

Pull down underwear and bottoms	Y	N
Sit on toilet seat	Y	N
Pee or poop in toilet	Y	N
Get tissue	Y	N
Wipe self with tissue	Y	N
Put tissue in toilet	Y	N
Pull up underwear and bottoms	Y	N
Flush the toilet	Y	N
Go to sink and turn on faucet	Y	N
Lather soap in hands for 20 sec.	Y	N
Rinse hands with water	Y	N
Turn off sink faucet	Y	N
Dry hands	Y	N

Directions: Mark Y if the skill is performed without assistance and N if the skill required assistance to be completed.

Date: /   /   Score:

I Can Use The Bathroom

Skill Progress Log

Pull down underwear and bottoms	Y	N
Sit on toilet seat	Y	N
Pee or poop in toilet	Y	N
Get tissue	Y	N
Wipe self with tissue	Y	N
Put tissue in toilet	Y	N
Pull up underwear and bottoms	Y	N
Flush the toilet	Y	N
Go to sink and turn on faucet	Y	N
Lather soap in hands for 20 sec.	Y	N
Rinse hands with water	Y	N
Turn off sink faucet	Y	N
Dry hands	Y	N

Directions: Mark Y if the skill is performed without assistance and N if the skill required assistance to be completed.

Date: / /   Score:

I Can Use The Bathroom

Skill Progress Log

Pull down underwear and bottoms	Y	N
Sit on toilet seat	Y	N
Pee or poop in toilet	Y	N
Get tissue	Y	N
Wipe self with tissue	Y	N
Put tissue in toilet	Y	N
Pull up underwear and bottoms	Y	N
Flush the toilet	Y	N
Go to sink and turn on faucet	Y	N
Lather soap in hands for 20 sec.	Y	N
Rinse hands with water	Y	N
Turn off sink faucet	Y	N
Dry hands	Y	N

Directions: Mark Y if the skill is performed without assistance and N if the skill required assistance to be completed.

Date: /   /   Score:

I Can Use The Bathroom

Skill Progress Log

Skill		
Pull down underwear and bottoms	Y	N
Sit on toilet seat	Y	N
Pee or poop in toilet	Y	N
Get tissue	Y	N
Wipe self with tissue	Y	N
Put tissue in toilet	Y	N
Pull up underwear and bottoms	Y	N
Flush the toilet	Y	N
Go to sink and turn on faucet	Y	N
Lather soap in hands for 20 sec.	Y	N
Rinse hands with water	Y	N
Turn off sink faucet	Y	N
Dry hands	Y	N

Directions: Mark Y if the skill is performed without assistance and N if the skill required assistance to be completed.

Date: / /   Score:

I Can Use The Bathroom

Skill Progress Log

Pull down underwear and bottoms	Y	N
Sit on toilet seat	Y	N
Pee or poop in toilet	Y	N
Get tissue	Y	N
Wipe self with tissue	Y	N
Put tissue in toilet	Y	N
Pull up underwear and bottoms	Y	N
Flush the toilet	Y	N
Go to sink and turn on faucet	Y	N
Lather soap in hands for 20 sec.	Y	N
Rinse hands with water	Y	N
Turn off sink faucet	Y	N
Dry hands	Y	N

Directions: Mark Y if the skill is performed without assistance and N if the skill required assistance to be completed.

Date: /   /   Score:

I Can Use The Bathroom

Skill Progress Log

Pull down underwear and bottoms	Y	N
Sit on toilet seat	Y	N
Pee or poop in toilet	Y	N
Get tissue	Y	N
Wipe self with tissue	Y	N
Put tissue in toilet	Y	N
Pull up underwear and bottoms	Y	N
Flush the toilet	Y	N
Go to sink and turn on faucet	Y	N
Lather soap in hands for 20 sec.	Y	N
Rinse hands with water	Y	N
Turn off sink faucet	Y	N
Dry hands	Y	N

Directions: Mark Y if the skill is performed without assistance and N if the skill required assistance to be completed.

Date: / /   Score:

I Can Use The Bathroom

Skill Progress Log

Pull down underwear and bottoms	Y	N
Sit on toilet seat	Y	N
Pee or poop in toilet	Y	N
Get tissue	Y	N
Wipe self with tissue	Y	N
Put tissue in toilet	Y	N
Pull up underwear and bottoms	Y	N
Flush the toilet	Y	N
Go to sink and turn on faucet	Y	N
Lather soap in hands for 20 sec.	Y	N
Rinse hands with water	Y	N
Turn off sink faucet	Y	N
Dry hands	Y	N

Directions: Mark Y if the skill is performed without assistance and N if the skill required assistance to be completed.

Date: / /   Score:

I Can Use The Bathroom

Skill Progress Log

Skill		
Pull down underwear and bottoms	Y	N
Sit on toilet seat	Y	N
Pee or poop in toilet	Y	N
Get tissue	Y	N
Wipe self with tissue	Y	N
Put tissue in toilet	Y	N
Pull up underwear and bottoms	Y	N
Flush the toilet	Y	N
Go to sink and turn on faucet	Y	N
Lather soap in hands for 20 sec.	Y	N
Rinse hands with water	Y	N
Turn off sink faucet	Y	N
Dry hands	Y	N

Directions: Mark Y if the skill is performed without assistance and N if the skill required assistance to be completed.

Date: / /   Score:

I Can Use The Bathroom

Skill Progress Log

Pull down underwear and bottoms	Y	N
Sit on toilet seat	Y	N
Pee or poop in toilet	Y	N
Get tissue	Y	N
Wipe self with tissue	Y	N
Put tissue in toilet	Y	N
Pull up underwear and bottoms	Y	N
Flush the toilet	Y	N
Go to sink and turn on faucet	Y	N
Lather soap in hands for 20 sec.	Y	N
Rinse hands with water	Y	N
Turn off sink faucet	Y	N
Dry hands	Y	N

Directions: Mark Y if the skill is performed without assistance and N if the skill required assistance to be completed.

Date: / / Score:

I Can Use The Bathroom

Skill Progress Log

Skill		
Pull down underwear and bottoms	Y	N
Sit on toilet seat	Y	N
Pee or poop in toilet	Y	N
Get tissue	Y	N
Wipe self with tissue	Y	N
Put tissue in toilet	Y	N
Pull up underwear and bottoms	Y	N
Flush the toilet	Y	N
Go to sink and turn on faucet	Y	N
Lather soap in hands for 20 sec.	Y	N
Rinse hands with water	Y	N
Turn off sink faucet	Y	N
Dry hands	Y	N

Directions: Mark Y if the skill is performed without assistance and N if the skill required assistance to be completed.

Date: /   /   Score:

I Can Use The Bathroom

Skill Progress Log

Skill		
Pull down underwear and bottoms	Y	N
Sit on toilet seat	Y	N
Pee or poop in toilet	Y	N
Get tissue	Y	N
Wipe self with tissue	Y	N
Put tissue in toilet	Y	N
Pull up underwear and bottoms	Y	N
Flush the toilet	Y	N
Go to sink and turn on faucet	Y	N
Lather soap in hands for 20 sec.	Y	N
Rinse hands with water	Y	N
Turn off sink faucet	Y	N
Dry hands	Y	N

Directions: Mark Y if the skill is performed without assistance and N if the skill required assistance to be completed.

Date: /   /   Score:

I Can Use The Bathroom

Skill Progress Log

Pull down underwear and bottoms	Y	N
Sit on toilet seat	Y	N
Pee or poop in toilet	Y	N
Get tissue	Y	N
Wipe self with tissue	Y	N
Put tissue in toilet	Y	N
Pull up underwear and bottoms	Y	N
Flush the toilet	Y	N
Go to sink and turn on faucet	Y	N
Lather soap in hands for 20 sec.	Y	N
Rinse hands with water	Y	N
Turn off sink faucet	Y	N
Dry hands	Y	N

Directions: Mark Y if the skill is performed without assistance and N if the skill required assistance to be completed.

Date: / /   Score:

I Can Use The Bathroom

Skill Progress Log

Pull down underwear and bottoms	Y	N
Sit on toilet seat	Y	N
Pee or poop in toilet	Y	N
Get tissue	Y	N
Wipe self with tissue	Y	N
Put tissue in toilet	Y	N
Pull up underwear and bottoms	Y	N
Flush the toilet	Y	N
Go to sink and turn on faucet	Y	N
Lather soap in hands for 20 sec.	Y	N
Rinse hands with water	Y	N
Turn off sink faucet	Y	N
Dry hands	Y	N

Directions: Mark Y if the skill is performed without assistance and N if the skill required assistance to be completed.

Date: /   /   Score:

I Can Use The Bathroom

Skill Progress Log

Pull down underwear and bottoms	Y	N
Sit on toilet seat	Y	N
Pee or poop in toilet	Y	N
Get tissue	Y	N
Wipe self with tissue	Y	N
Put tissue in toilet	Y	N
Pull up underwear and bottoms	Y	N
Flush the toilet	Y	N
Go to sink and turn on faucet	Y	N
Lather soap in hands for 20 sec.	Y	N
Rinse hands with water	Y	N
Turn off sink faucet	Y	N
Dry hands	Y	N

Directions: Mark Y if the skill is performed without assistance and N if the skill required assistance to be completed.

Date: /   /   Score:

I Can Use The Bathroom

Skill Progress Log

Skill		
Pull down underwear and bottoms	Y	N
Sit on toilet seat	Y	N
Pee or poop in toilet	Y	N
Get tissue	Y	N
Wipe self with tissue	Y	N
Put tissue in toilet	Y	N
Pull up underwear and bottoms	Y	N
Flush the toilet	Y	N
Go to sink and turn on faucet	Y	N
Lather soap in hands for 20 sec.	Y	N
Rinse hands with water	Y	N
Turn off sink faucet	Y	N
Dry hands	Y	N

Directions: Mark Y if the skill is performed without assistance and N if the skill required assistance to be completed.

Date: / /   Score:

I Can Use The Bathroom

Skill Progress Log

Skill		
Pull down underwear and bottoms	Y	N
Sit on toilet seat	Y	N
Pee or poop in toilet	Y	N
Get tissue	Y	N
Wipe self with tissue	Y	N
Put tissue in toilet	Y	N
Pull up underwear and bottoms	Y	N
Flush the toilet	Y	N
Go to sink and turn on faucet	Y	N
Lather soap in hands for 20 sec.	Y	N
Rinse hands with water	Y	N
Turn off sink faucet	Y	N
Dry hands	Y	N

Directions: Mark Y if the skill is performed without assistance and N if the skill required assistance to be completed.

Date: / /   Score:

I Can Use The Bathroom

Skill Progress Log

Skill		
Pull down underwear and bottoms	Y	N
Sit on toilet seat	Y	N
Pee or poop in toilet	Y	N
Get tissue	Y	N
Wipe self with tissue	Y	N
Put tissue in toilet	Y	N
Pull up underwear and bottoms	Y	N
Flush the toilet	Y	N
Go to sink and turn on faucet	Y	N
Lather soap in hands for 20 sec.	Y	N
Rinse hands with water	Y	N
Turn off sink faucet	Y	N
Dry hands	Y	N

Directions: Mark Y if the skill is performed without assistance and N if the skill required assistance to be completed.

Date: /   /   Score:

I Can Use The Bathroom

Skill Progress Log

Pull down underwear and bottoms	Y	N
Sit on toilet seat	Y	N
Pee or poop in toilet	Y	N
Get tissue	Y	N
Wipe self with tissue	Y	N
Put tissue in toilet	Y	N
Pull up underwear and bottoms	Y	N
Flush the toilet	Y	N
Go to sink and turn on faucet	Y	N
Lather soap in hands for 20 sec.	Y	N
Rinse hands with water	Y	N
Turn off sink faucet	Y	N
Dry hands	Y	N

Directions: Mark Y if the skill is performed without assistance and N if the skill required assistance to be completed.

Date: /   /   Score:

I Can Use The Bathroom

Skill Progress Log

Skill		
Pull down underwear and bottoms	Y	N
Sit on toilet seat	Y	N
Pee or poop in toilet	Y	N
Get tissue	Y	N
Wipe self with tissue	Y	N
Put tissue in toilet	Y	N
Pull up underwear and bottoms	Y	N
Flush the toilet	Y	N
Go to sink and turn on faucet	Y	N
Lather soap in hands for 20 sec.	Y	N
Rinse hands with water	Y	N
Turn off sink faucet	Y	N
Dry hands	Y	N

Directions: Mark Y if the skill is performed without assistance and N if the skill required assistance to be completed.

Date: / /   Score:

I Can Use The Bathroom

Skill Progress Log

Skill		
Pull down underwear and bottoms	Y	N
Sit on toilet seat	Y	N
Pee or poop in toilet	Y	N
Get tissue	Y	N
Wipe self with tissue	Y	N
Put tissue in toilet	Y	N
Pull up underwear and bottoms	Y	N
Flush the toilet	Y	N
Go to sink and turn on faucet	Y	N
Lather soap in hands for 20 sec.	Y	N
Rinse hands with water	Y	N
Turn off sink faucet	Y	N
Dry hands	Y	N

Directions: Mark Y if the skill is performed without assistance and N if the skill required assistance to be completed.

Date   /   /   Score:

I Can Use The Bathroom

Skill Progress Log

Pull down underwear and bottoms	Y	N
Sit on toilet seat	Y	N
Pee or poop in toilet	Y	N
Get tissue	Y	N
Wipe self with tissue	Y	N
Put tissue in toilet	Y	N
Pull up underwear and bottoms	Y	N
Flush the toilet	Y	N
Go to sink and turn on faucet	Y	N
Lather soap in hands for 20 sec.	Y	N
Rinse hands with water	Y	N
Turn off sink faucet	Y	N
Dry hands	Y	N

Directions: Mark Y if the skill is performed without assistance and N if the skill required assistance to be completed.

Date: /   /   Score:

I Can Wash My Hands

Skill Progress Log

Go to the bathroom	Y	N
Go to the sink	Y	N
Turn on sink faucet	Y	N
Wet hands	Y	N
Apply soap to hands	Y	N
Lather soap in hands for 20 sec.	Y	N
Rinse hands	Y	N
Turn off sink faucet	Y	N
Get a towel	Y	N
Dry hands	Y	N

Directions: Mark Y if the skill is performed without assistance and N if the skill required assistance to be completed.

Date: / /   Score:

I Can Wash My Hands

Skill Progress Log

Go to the bathroom	Y	N
Go to the sink	Y	N
Turn on sink faucet	Y	N
Wet hands	Y	N
Apply soap to hands	Y	N
Lather soap in hands for 20 sec.	Y	N
Rinse hands	Y	N
Turn off sink faucet	Y	N
Get a towel	Y	N
Dry hands	Y	N

Directions: Mark Y if the skill is performed without assistance and N if the skill required assistance to be completed.

Date: / /   Score:

I Can Wash My Hands

Skill Progress Log

Go to the bathroom	Y	N
Go to the sink	Y	N
Turn on sink faucet	Y	N
Wet hands	Y	N
Apply soap to hands	Y	N
Lather soap in hands for 20 sec.	Y	N
Rinse hands	Y	N
Turn off sink faucet	Y	N
Get a towel	Y	N
Dry hands	Y	N

Directions: Mark Y if the skill is performed without assistance and N if the skill required assistance to be completed.

Date: / /   Score:

I Can Wash My Hands

Skill Progress Log

Go to the bathroom	Y	N
Go to the sink	Y	N
Turn on sink faucet	Y	N
Wet hands	Y	N
Apply soap to hands	Y	N
Lather soap in hands for 20 sec.	Y	N
Rinse hands	Y	N
Turn off sink faucet	Y	N
Get a towel	Y	N
Dry hands	Y	N

Directions: Mark Y if the skill is performed without assistance and N if the skill required assistance to be completed.

Date: / /   Score:

I Can Wash My Hands

Skill Progress Log

Go to the bathroom	Y	N
Go to the sink	Y	N
Turn on sink faucet	Y	N
Wet hands	Y	N
Apply soap to hands	Y	N
Lather soap in hands for 20 sec.	Y	N
Rinse hands	Y	N
Turn off sink faucet	Y	N
Get a towel	Y	N
Dry hands	Y	N

Directions: Mark Y if the skill is performed without assistance and N if the skill required assistance to be completed.

Date: /   /   Score:

I Can Wash My Hands

Skill Progress Log

Go to the bathroom	Y	N
Go to the sink	Y	N
Turn on sink faucet	Y	N
Wet hands	Y	N
Apply soap to hands	Y	N
Lather soap in hands for 20 sec.	Y	N
Rinse hands	Y	N
Turn off sink faucet	Y	N
Get a towel	Y	N
Dry hands	Y	N

Directions: Mark Y if the skill is performed without assistance and N if the skill required assistance to be completed.

Date: / /   Score:

I Can Wash My Hands

Skill Progress Log

Go to the bathroom	Y	N
Go to the sink	Y	N
Turn on sink faucet	Y	N
Wet hands	Y	N
Apply soap to hands	Y	N
Lather soap in hands for 20 sec.	Y	N
Rinse hands	Y	N
Turn off sink faucet	Y	N
Get a towel	Y	N
Dry hands	Y	N

Directions: Mark Y if the skill is performed without assistance and N if the skill required assistance to be completed.

Date: /   /   Score:

I Can Wash My Hands

Skill Progress Log

Go to the bathroom	Y	N
Go to the sink	Y	N
Turn on sink faucet	Y	N
Wet hands	Y	N
Apply soap to hands	Y	N
Lather soap in hands for 20 sec.	Y	N
Rinse hands	Y	N
Turn off sink faucet	Y	N
Get a towel	Y	N
Dry hands	Y	N

Directions: Mark Y if the skill is performed without assistance and N if the skill required assistance to be completed.

Date: / / Score:

I Can Wash My Hands

Skill Progress Log

Go to the bathroom	Y	N
Go to the sink	Y	N
Turn on sink faucet	Y	N
Wet hands	Y	N
Apply soap to hands	Y	N
Lather soap in hands for 20 sec.	Y	N
Rinse hands	Y	N
Turn off sink faucet	Y	N
Get a towel	Y	N
Dry hands	Y	N

Directions: Mark Y if the skill is performed without assistance and N if the skill required assistance to be completed.

Date: /   /   Score:

I Can Wash My Hands

Skill Progress Log

Go to the bathroom	Y	N
Go to the sink	Y	N
Turn on sink faucet	Y	N
Wet hands	Y	N
Apply soap to hands	Y	N
Lather soap in hands for 20 sec.	Y	N
Rinse hands	Y	N
Turn off sink faucet	Y	N
Get a towel	Y	N
Dry hands	Y	N

Directions: Mark Y if the skill is performed without assistance and N if the skill required assistance to be completed.

Date: /   /   Score:

I Can Wash My Hands

Skill Progress Log

Go to the bathroom	Y	N
Go to the sink	Y	N
Turn on sink faucet	Y	N
Wet hands	Y	N
Apply soap to hands	Y	N
Lather soap in hands for 20 sec.	Y	N
Rinse hands	Y	N
Turn off sink faucet	Y	N
Get a towel	Y	N
Dry hands	Y	N

Directions: Mark Y if the skill is performed without assistance and N if the skill required assistance to be completed.

Date: /   /   Score:

I Can Wash My Hands

Skill Progress Log

Go to the bathroom	Y	N
Go to the sink	Y	N
Turn on sink faucet	Y	N
Wet hands	Y	N
Apply soap to hands	Y	N
Lather soap in hands for 20 sec.	Y	N
Rinse hands	Y	N
Turn off sink faucet	Y	N
Get a towel	Y	N
Dry hands	Y	N

Directions: Mark Y if the skill is performed without assistance and N if the skill required assistance to be completed.

Date: / /   Score:

I Can Wash My Hands

Skill Progress Log

Go to the bathroom	Y	N
Go to the sink	Y	N
Turn on sink faucet	Y	N
Wet hands	Y	N
Apply soap to hands	Y	N
Lather soap in hands for 20 sec.	Y	N
Rinse hands	Y	N
Turn off sink faucet	Y	N
Get a towel	Y	N
Dry hands	Y	N

Directions: Mark Y if the skill is performed without assistance and N if the skill required assistance to be completed.

Date: / /   Score:

I Can Wash My Hands

Skill Progress Log

Go to the bathroom	Y	N
Go to the sink	Y	N
Turn on sink faucet	Y	N
Wet hands	Y	N
Apply soap to hands	Y	N
Lather soap in hands for 20 sec.	Y	N
Rinse hands	Y	N
Turn off sink faucet	Y	N
Get a towel	Y	N
Dry hands	Y	N

Directions: Mark Y if the skill is performed without assistance and N if the skill required assistance to be completed.

Date: / /   Score:

I Can Wash My Hands

Skill Progress Log

Go to the bathroom	Y	N
Go to the sink	Y	N
Turn on sink faucet	Y	N
Wet hands	Y	N
Apply soap to hands	Y	N
Lather soap in hands for 20 sec.	Y	N
Rinse hands	Y	N
Turn off sink faucet	Y	N
Get a towel	Y	N
Dry hands	Y	N

Directions: Mark Y if the skill is performed without assistance and N if the skill required assistance to be completed.

Date: /   /   Score:

I Can Wash My Hands

Skill Progress Log

Go to the bathroom	Y	N
Go to the sink	Y	N
Turn on sink faucet	Y	N
Wet hands	Y	N
Apply soap to hands	Y	N
Lather soap in hands for 20 sec.	Y	N
Rinse hands	Y	N
Turn off sink faucet	Y	N
Get a towel	Y	N
Dry hands	Y	N

Directions: Mark Y if the skill is performed without assistance and N if the skill required assistance to be completed.

Date: / /   Score:

I Can Wash My Hands

Skill Progress Log

Go to the bathroom	Y	N
Go to the sink	Y	N
Turn on sink faucet	Y	N
Wet hands	Y	N
Apply soap to hands	Y	N
Lather soap in hands for 20 sec.	Y	N
Rinse hands	Y	N
Turn off sink faucet	Y	N
Get a towel	Y	N
Dry hands	Y	N

Directions: Mark Y if the skill is performed without assistance and N if the skill required assistance to be completed.

Date: /   /   Score:

I Can Wash My Hands

Skill Progress Log

Go to the bathroom	Y	N
Go to the sink	Y	N
Turn on sink faucet	Y	N
Wet hands	Y	N
Apply soap to hands	Y	N
Lather soap in hands for 20 sec.	Y	N
Rinse hands	Y	N
Turn off sink faucet	Y	N
Get a towel	Y	N
Dry hands	Y	N

Directions: Mark Y if the skill is performed without assistance and N if the skill required assistance to be completed.

Date: /   /   Score:

I Can Wash My Hands

Skill Progress Log

Go to the bathroom	Y	N
Go to the sink	Y	N
Turn on sink faucet	Y	N
Wet hands	Y	N
Apply soap to hands	Y	N
Lather soap in hands for 20 sec.	Y	N
Rinse hands	Y	N
Turn off sink faucet	Y	N
Get a towel	Y	N
Dry hands	Y	N

Directions: Mark Y if the skill is performed without assistance and N if the skill required assistance to be completed.

Date: /   /   Score:

I Can Wash My Hands

Skill Progress Log

Go to the bathroom	Y	N
Go to the sink	Y	N
Turn on sink faucet	Y	N
Wet hands	Y	N
Apply soap to hands	Y	N
Lather soap in hands for 20 sec.	Y	N
Rinse hands	Y	N
Turn off sink faucet	Y	N
Get a towel	Y	N
Dry hands	Y	N

Directions: Mark Y if the skill is performed without assistance and N if the skill required assistance to be completed.

Date: / /   Score:

I Can Wash My Hands

Skill Progress Log

Go to the bathroom	Y	N
Go to the sink	Y	N
Turn on sink faucet	Y	N
Wet hands	Y	N
Apply soap to hands	Y	N
Lather soap in hands for 20 sec.	Y	N
Rinse hands	Y	N
Turn off sink faucet	Y	N
Get a towel	Y	N
Dry hands	Y	N

Directions: Mark Y if the skill is performed without assistance and N if the skill required assistance to be completed.

Date: / /   Score:

I Can Wash My Hands

Skill Progress Log

Go to the bathroom	Y	N
Go to the sink	Y	N
Turn on sink faucet	Y	N
Wet hands	Y	N
Apply soap to hands	Y	N
Lather soap in hands for 20 sec.	Y	N
Rinse hands	Y	N
Turn off sink faucet	Y	N
Get a towel	Y	N
Dry hands	Y	N

Directions: Mark Y if the skill is performed without assistance and N if the skill required assistance to be completed.

Date: / /   Score:

I Can Wash My Hands

Skill Progress Log

Go to the bathroom	Y	N
Go to the sink	Y	N
Turn on sink faucet	Y	N
Wet hands	Y	N
Apply soap to hands	Y	N
Lather soap in hands for 20 sec.	Y	N
Rinse hands	Y	N
Turn off sink faucet	Y	N
Get a towel	Y	N
Dry hands	Y	N

Directions: Mark Y if the skill is performed without assistance and N if the skill required assistance to be completed.

Date: / /   Score:

I Can Wash My Hands

Skill Progress Log

Go to the bathroom	Y	N
Go to the sink	Y	N
Turn on sink faucet	Y	N
Wet hands	Y	N
Apply soap to hands	Y	N
Lather soap in hands for 20 sec.	Y	N
Rinse hands	Y	N
Turn off sink faucet	Y	N
Get a towel	Y	N
Dry hands	Y	N

Directions: Mark Y if the skill is performed without assistance and N if the skill required assistance to be completed.

Date: / /   Score:

I Can Wash My Hands

Skill Progress Log

Go to the bathroom	Y	N
Go to the sink	Y	N
Turn on sink faucet	Y	N
Wet hands	Y	N
Apply soap to hands	Y	N
Lather soap in hands for 20 sec.	Y	N
Rinse hands	Y	N
Turn off sink faucet	Y	N
Get a towel	Y	N
Dry hands	Y	N

Directions: Mark Y if the skill is performed without assistance and N if the skill required assistance to be completed.

Date: /   /   Score:

I Can Wash My Hands

Skill Progress Log

Go to the bathroom	Y	N
Go to the sink	Y	N
Turn on sink faucet	Y	N
Wet hands	Y	N
Apply soap to hands	Y	N
Lather soap in hands for 20 sec.	Y	N
Rinse hands	Y	N
Turn off sink faucet	Y	N
Get a towel	Y	N
Dry hands	Y	N

Directions: Mark Y if the skill is performed without assistance and N if the skill required assistance to be completed.

Date: /   /   Score:

I Can Wash My Hands

Skill Progress Log

Go to the bathroom	Y	N
Go to the sink	Y	N
Turn on sink faucet	Y	N
Wet hands	Y	N
Apply soap to hands	Y	N
Lather soap in hands for 20 sec.	Y	N
Rinse hands	Y	N
Turn off sink faucet	Y	N
Get a towel	Y	N
Dry hands	Y	N

Directions: Mark Y if the skill is performed without assistance and N if the skill required assistance to be completed.

Date: /   /   Score:

I Can Wash My Hands

Skill Progress Log

Go to the bathroom	Y	N
Go to the sink	Y	N
Turn on sink faucet	Y	N
Wet hands	Y	N
Apply soap to hands	Y	N
Lather soap in hands for 20 sec.	Y	N
Rinse hands	Y	N
Turn off sink faucet	Y	N
Get a towel	Y	N
Dry hands	Y	N

Directions: Mark Y if the skill is performed without assistance and N if the skill required assistance to be completed.

Date: / /   Score:

I Can Wash My Hands

Skill Progress Log

Go to the bathroom	Y	N
Go to the sink	Y	N
Turn on sink faucet	Y	N
Wet hands	Y	N
Apply soap to hands	Y	N
Lather soap in hands for 20 sec.	Y	N
Rinse hands	Y	N
Turn off sink faucet	Y	N
Get a towel	Y	N
Dry hands	Y	N

Directions: Mark Y if the skill is performed without assistance and N if the skill required assistance to be completed.

Date: / /   Score:

I Can Wash My Hands

Skill Progress Log

Go to the bathroom	Y	N
Go to the sink	Y	N
Turn on sink faucet	Y	N
Wet hands	Y	N
Apply soap to hands	Y	N
Lather soap in hands for 20 sec.	Y	N
Rinse hands	Y	N
Turn off sink faucet	Y	N
Get a towel	Y	N
Dry hands	Y	N

Directions: Mark Y if the skill is performed without assistance and N if the skill required assistance to be completed.

Date: /   /   Score:

I Can Wash My Hands

Skill Progress Log

Go to the bathroom	Y	N
Go to the sink	Y	N
Turn on sink faucet	Y	N
Wet hands	Y	N
Apply soap to hands	Y	N
Lather soap in hands for 20 sec.	Y	N
Rinse hands	Y	N
Turn off sink faucet	Y	N
Get a towel	Y	N
Dry hands	Y	N

Directions: Mark Y if the skill is performed without assistance and N if the skill required assistance to be completed.

Date: / /   Score:

I Can Brush My Teeth

Skill Progress Log

Attain toothbrush and toothpaste	Y	N
Turn on sink faucet	Y	N
Wet toothbrush	Y	N
Put toothpaste on toothbrush	Y	N
Brush front teeth	Y	N
Brush teeth on right side	Y	N
Brush teeth on left side	Y	N
Brush bottom teeth	Y	N
Brush tongue	Y	N
Rinse toothbrush with water	Y	N
Rinse mouth with water	Y	N
Spit into the sink	Y	N
Turn off sink faucet	Y	N

Directions: Mark Y if the skill is performed without assistance and N if the skill required assistance to be completed.

Date: / /   Score:

I Can Brush My Teeth

Skill Progress Log

Attain toothbrush and toothpaste	Y	N
Turn on sink faucet	Y	N
Wet toothbrush	Y	N
Put toothpaste on toothbrush	Y	N
Brush front teeth	Y	N
Brush teeth on right side	Y	N
Brush teeth on left side	Y	N
Brush bottom teeth	Y	N
Brush tongue	Y	N
Rinse toothbrush with water	Y	N
Rinse mouth with water	Y	N
Spit into the sink	Y	N
Turn off sink faucet	Y	N

Directions: Mark Y if the skill is performed without assistance and N if the skill required assistance to be completed.

Date: / /   Score:

I Can Brush My Teeth

Skill Progress Log

Attain toothbrush and toothpaste	Y	N
Turn on sink faucet	Y	N
Wet toothbrush	Y	N
Put toothpaste on toothbrush	Y	N
Brush front teeth	Y	N
Brush teeth on right side	Y	N
Brush teeth on left side	Y	N
Brush bottom teeth	Y	N
Brush tongue	Y	N
Rinse toothbrush with water	Y	N
Rinse mouth with water	Y	N
Spit into the sink	Y	N
Turn off sink faucet	Y	N

Directions: Mark Y if the skill is performed without assistance and N if the skill required assistance to be completed.

Date: /   /   Score:

I Can Brush My Teeth

Skill Progress Log

Attain toothbrush and toothpaste	Y	N
Turn on sink faucet	Y	N
Wet toothbrush	Y	N
Put toothpaste on toothbrush	Y	N
Brush front teeth	Y	N
Brush teeth on right side	Y	N
Brush teeth on left side	Y	N
Brush bottom teeth	Y	N
Brush tongue	Y	N
Rinse toothbrush with water	Y	N
Rinse mouth with water	Y	N
Spit into the sink	Y	N
Turn off sink faucet	Y	N

Directions: Mark Y if the skill is performed without assistance and N if the skill required assistance to be completed.

Date: /   /   Score:

I Can Brush My Teeth

Skill Progress Log

Attain toothbrush and toothpaste	Y	N
Turn on sink faucet	Y	N
Wet toothbrush	Y	N
Put toothpaste on toothbrush	Y	N
Brush front teeth	Y	N
Brush teeth on right side	Y	N
Brush teeth on left side	Y	N
Brush bottom teeth	Y	N
Brush tongue	Y	N
Rinse toothbrush with water	Y	N
Rinse mouth with water	Y	N
Spit into the sink	Y	N
Turn off sink faucet	Y	N

Directions: Mark Y if the skill is performed without assistance and N if the skill required assistance to be completed.

Date: /   /   Score:

I Can Brush My Teeth

Skill Progress Log

Attain toothbrush and toothpaste	Y	N
Turn on sink faucet	Y	N
Wet toothbrush	Y	N
Put toothpaste on toothbrush	Y	N
Brush front teeth	Y	N
Brush teeth on right side	Y	N
Brush teeth on left side	Y	N
Brush bottom teeth	Y	N
Brush tongue	Y	N
Rinse toothbrush with water	Y	N
Rinse mouth with water	Y	N
Spit into the sink	Y	N
Turn off sink faucet	Y	N

Directions: Mark Y if the skill is performed without assistance and N if the skill required assistance to be completed.

Date: / /   Score:

I Can Brush My Teeth

Skill Progress Log

Attain toothbrush and toothpaste	Y	N
Turn on sink faucet	Y	N
Wet toothbrush	Y	N
Put toothpaste on toothbrush	Y	N
Brush front teeth	Y	N
Brush teeth on right side	Y	N
Brush teeth on left side	Y	N
Brush bottom teeth	Y	N
Brush tongue	Y	N
Rinse toothbrush with water	Y	N
Rinse mouth with water	Y	N
Spit into the sink	Y	N
Turn off sink faucet	Y	N

Directions: Mark Y if the skill is performed without assistance and N if the skill required assistance to be completed.

Date: /   /   Score:

I Can Brush My Teeth

Skill Progress Log

Attain toothbrush and toothpaste	Y	N
Turn on sink faucet	Y	N
Wet toothbrush	Y	N
Put toothpaste on toothbrush	Y	N
Brush front teeth	Y	N
Brush teeth on right side	Y	N
Brush teeth on left side	Y	N
Brush bottom teeth	Y	N
Brush tongue	Y	N
Rinse toothbrush with water	Y	N
Rinse mouth with water	Y	N
Spit into the sink	Y	N
Turn off sink faucet	Y	N

Directions: Mark Y if the skill is performed without assistance and N if the skill required assistance to be completed.

Date: / /   Score:

I Can Brush My Teeth

Skill Progress Log

Attain toothbrush and toothpaste	Y	N
Turn on sink faucet	Y	N
Wet toothbrush	Y	N
Put toothpaste on toothbrush	Y	N
Brush front teeth	Y	N
Brush teeth on right side	Y	N
Brush teeth on left side	Y	N
Brush bottom teeth	Y	N
Brush tongue	Y	N
Rinse toothbrush with water	Y	N
Rinse mouth with water	Y	N
Spit into the sink	Y	N
Turn off sink faucet	Y	N

Directions: Mark Y if the skill is performed without assistance and N if the skill required assistance to be completed.

Date: /   /   Score:

I Can Brush My Teeth

Skill Progress Log

Attain toothbrush and toothpaste	Y	N
Turn on sink faucet	Y	N
Wet toothbrush	Y	N
Put toothpaste on toothbrush	Y	N
Brush front teeth	Y	N
Brush teeth on right side	Y	N
Brush teeth on left side	Y	N
Brush bottom teeth	Y	N
Brush tongue	Y	N
Rinse toothbrush with water	Y	N
Rinse mouth with water	Y	N
Spit into the sink	Y	N
Turn off sink faucet	Y	N

Directions: Mark Y if the skill is performed without assistance and N if the skill required assistance to be completed.

Date: /   /   Score:

I Can Brush My Teeth

Skill Progress Log

Attain toothbrush and toothpaste	Y	N
Turn on sink faucet	Y	N
Wet toothbrush	Y	N
Put toothpaste on toothbrush	Y	N
Brush front teeth	Y	N
Brush teeth on right side	Y	N
Brush teeth on left side	Y	N
Brush bottom teeth	Y	N
Brush tongue	Y	N
Rinse toothbrush with water	Y	N
Rinse mouth with water	Y	N
Spit into the sink	Y	N
Turn off sink faucet	Y	N

Directions: Mark Y if the skill is performed without assistance and N if the skill required assistance to be completed.

Date: /   /   Score:

I Can Brush My Teeth

Skill Progress Log

Attain toothbrush and toothpaste	Y	N
Turn on sink faucet	Y	N
Wet toothbrush	Y	N
Put toothpaste on toothbrush	Y	N
Brush front teeth	Y	N
Brush teeth on right side	Y	N
Brush teeth on left side	Y	N
Brush bottom teeth	Y	N
Brush tongue	Y	N
Rinse toothbrush with water	Y	N
Rinse mouth with water	Y	N
Spit into the sink	Y	N
Turn off sink faucet	Y	N

Directions: Mark Y if the skill is performed without assistance and N if the skill required assistance to be completed.

Date: /   /   Score:

I Can Brush My Teeth

Skill Progress Log

Attain toothbrush and toothpaste	Y	N
Turn on sink faucet	Y	N
Wet toothbrush	Y	N
Put toothpaste on toothbrush	Y	N
Brush front teeth	Y	N
Brush teeth on right side	Y	N
Brush teeth on left side	Y	N
Brush bottom teeth	Y	N
Brush tongue	Y	N
Rinse toothbrush with water	Y	N
Rinse mouth with water	Y	N
Spit into the sink	Y	N
Turn off sink faucet	Y	N

Directions: Mark Y if the skill is performed without assistance and N if the skill required assistance to be completed.

Date: /   /   Score:

I Can Brush My Teeth

Skill Progress Log

Attain toothbrush and toothpaste	Y	N
Turn on sink faucet	Y	N
Wet toothbrush	Y	N
Put toothpaste on toothbrush	Y	N
Brush front teeth	Y	N
Brush teeth on right side	Y	N
Brush teeth on left side	Y	N
Brush bottom teeth	Y	N
Brush tongue	Y	N
Rinse toothbrush with water	Y	N
Rinse mouth with water	Y	N
Spit into the sink	Y	N
Turn off sink faucet	Y	N

Directions: Mark Y if the skill is performed without assistance and N if the skill required assistance to be completed.

Date: / /   Score:

I Can Brush My Teeth

Skill Progress Log

Attain toothbrush and toothpaste	Y	N
Turn on sink faucet	Y	N
Wet toothbrush	Y	N
Put toothpaste on toothbrush	Y	N
Brush front teeth	Y	N
Brush teeth on right side	Y	N
Brush teeth on left side	Y	N
Brush bottom teeth	Y	N
Brush tongue	Y	N
Rinse toothbrush with water	Y	N
Rinse mouth with water	Y	N
Spit into the sink	Y	N
Turn off sink faucet	Y	N

Directions: Mark Y if the skill is performed without assistance and N if the skill required assistance to be completed.

Date: / /   Score:

I Can Brush My Teeth

Skill Progress Log

Attain toothbrush and toothpaste	Y	N
Turn on sink faucet	Y	N
Wet toothbrush	Y	N
Put toothpaste on toothbrush	Y	N
Brush front teeth	Y	N
Brush teeth on right side	Y	N
Brush teeth on left side	Y	N
Brush bottom teeth	Y	N
Brush tongue	Y	N
Rinse toothbrush with water	Y	N
Rinse mouth with water	Y	N
Spit into the sink	Y	N
Turn off sink faucet	Y	N

Directions: Mark Y if the skill is performed without assistance and N if the skill required assistance to be completed.

Date: / /   Score:

I Can Brush My Teeth

Skill Progress Log

Attain toothbrush and toothpaste	Y	N
Turn on sink faucet	Y	N
Wet toothbrush	Y	N
Put toothpaste on toothbrush	Y	N
Brush front teeth	Y	N
Brush teeth on right side	Y	N
Brush teeth on left side	Y	N
Brush bottom teeth	Y	N
Brush tongue	Y	N
Rinse toothbrush with water	Y	N
Rinse mouth with water	Y	N
Spit into the sink	Y	N
Turn off sink faucet	Y	N

Directions: Mark Y if the skill is performed without assistance and N if the skill required assistance to be completed.

Date: / /   Score:

I Can Brush My Teeth

Skill Progress Log

Attain toothbrush and toothpaste	Y	N
Turn on sink faucet	Y	N
Wet toothbrush	Y	N
Put toothpaste on toothbrush	Y	N
Brush front teeth	Y	N
Brush teeth on right side	Y	N
Brush teeth on left side	Y	N
Brush bottom teeth	Y	N
Brush tongue	Y	N
Rinse toothbrush with water	Y	N
Rinse mouth with water	Y	N
Spit into the sink	Y	N
Turn off sink faucet	Y	N

Directions: Mark Y if the skill is performed without assistance and N if the skill required assistance to be completed.

Date: /   /   Score:

I Can Brush My Teeth

Skill Progress Log

Attain toothbrush and toothpaste	Y	N
Turn on sink faucet	Y	N
Wet toothbrush	Y	N
Put toothpaste on toothbrush	Y	N
Brush front teeth	Y	N
Brush teeth on right side	Y	N
Brush teeth on left side	Y	N
Brush bottom teeth	Y	N
Brush tongue	Y	N
Rinse toothbrush with water	Y	N
Rinse mouth with water	Y	N
Spit into the sink	Y	N
Turn off sink faucet	Y	N

Directions: Mark Y if the skill is performed without assistance and N if the skill required assistance to be completed.

Date: /   /   Score:

I Can Brush My Teeth

Skill Progress Log

Attain toothbrush and toothpaste	Y	N
Turn on sink faucet	Y	N
Wet toothbrush	Y	N
Put toothpaste on toothbrush	Y	N
Brush front teeth	Y	N
Brush teeth on right side	Y	N
Brush teeth on left side	Y	N
Brush bottom teeth	Y	N
Brush tongue	Y	N
Rinse toothbrush with water	Y	N
Rinse mouth with water	Y	N
Spit into the sink	Y	N
Turn off sink faucet	Y	N

Directions: Mark Y if the skill is performed without assistance and N if the skill required assistance to be completed.

Date: / /   Score:

I Can Brush My Teeth

Skill Progress Log

Attain toothbrush and toothpaste	Y	N
Turn on sink faucet	Y	N
Wet toothbrush	Y	N
Put toothpaste on toothbrush	Y	N
Brush front teeth	Y	N
Brush teeth on right side	Y	N
Brush teeth on left side	Y	N
Brush bottom teeth	Y	N
Brush tongue	Y	N
Rinse toothbrush with water	Y	N
Rinse mouth with water	Y	N
Spit into the sink	Y	N
Turn off sink faucet	Y	N

Directions: Mark Y if the skill is performed without assistance and N if the skill required assistance to be completed.

Date: / /   Score:

I Can Brush My Teeth

Skill Progress Log

Attain toothbrush and toothpaste	Y	N
Turn on sink faucet	Y	N
Wet toothbrush	Y	N
Put toothpaste on toothbrush	Y	N
Brush front teeth	Y	N
Brush teeth on right side	Y	N
Brush teeth on left side	Y	N
Brush bottom teeth	Y	N
Brush tongue	Y	N
Rinse toothbrush with water	Y	N
Rinse mouth with water	Y	N
Spit into the sink	Y	N
Turn off sink faucet	Y	N

Directions: Mark Y if the skill is performed without assistance and N if the skill required assistance to be completed.

Date: /   /   Score:

I Can Brush My Teeth

Skill Progress Log

Attain toothbrush and toothpaste	Y	N
Turn on sink faucet	Y	N
Wet toothbrush	Y	N
Put toothpaste on toothbrush	Y	N
Brush front teeth	Y	N
Brush teeth on right side	Y	N
Brush teeth on left side	Y	N
Brush bottom teeth	Y	N
Brush tongue	Y	N
Rinse toothbrush with water	Y	N
Rinse mouth with water	Y	N
Spit into the sink	Y	N
Turn off sink faucet	Y	N

Directions: Mark Y if the skill is performed without assistance and N if the skill required assistance to be completed.

Date: /   /   Score:

I Can Brush My Teeth

Skill Progress Log

Attain toothbrush and toothpaste	Y	N
Turn on sink faucet	Y	N
Wet toothbrush	Y	N
Put toothpaste on toothbrush	Y	N
Brush front teeth	Y	N
Brush teeth on right side	Y	N
Brush teeth on left side	Y	N
Brush bottom teeth	Y	N
Brush tongue	Y	N
Rinse toothbrush with water	Y	N
Rinse mouth with water	Y	N
Spit into the sink	Y	N
Turn off sink faucet	Y	N

Directions: Mark Y if the skill is performed without assistance and N if the skill required assistance to be completed.

Date: / /   Score:

I Can Brush My Teeth

Skill Progress Log

Attain toothbrush and toothpaste	Y	N
Turn on sink faucet	Y	N
Wet toothbrush	Y	N
Put toothpaste on toothbrush	Y	N
Brush front teeth	Y	N
Brush teeth on right side	Y	N
Brush teeth on left side	Y	N
Brush bottom teeth	Y	N
Brush tongue	Y	N
Rinse toothbrush with water	Y	N
Rinse mouth with water	Y	N
Spit into the sink	Y	N
Turn off sink faucet	Y	N

Directions: Mark Y if the skill is performed without assistance and N if the skill required assistance to be completed.

Date: /   /   Score:

I Can Brush My Teeth

Skill Progress Log

Attain toothbrush and toothpaste	Y	N
Turn on sink faucet	Y	N
Wet toothbrush	Y	N
Put toothpaste on toothbrush	Y	N
Brush front teeth	Y	N
Brush teeth on right side	Y	N
Brush teeth on left side	Y	N
Brush bottom teeth	Y	N
Brush tongue	Y	N
Rinse toothbrush with water	Y	N
Rinse mouth with water	Y	N
Spit into the sink	Y	N
Turn off sink faucet	Y	N

Directions: Mark Y if the skill is performed without assistance and N if the skill required assistance to be completed.

Date: / /   Score:

I Can Brush My Teeth

Skill Progress Log

Attain toothbrush and toothpaste	Y	N
Turn on sink faucet	Y	N
Wet toothbrush	Y	N
Put toothpaste on toothbrush	Y	N
Brush front teeth	Y	N
Brush teeth on right side	Y	N
Brush teeth on left side	Y	N
Brush bottom teeth	Y	N
Brush tongue	Y	N
Rinse toothbrush with water	Y	N
Rinse mouth with water	Y	N
Spit into the sink	Y	N
Turn off sink faucet	Y	N

Directions: Mark Y if the skill is performed without assistance and N if the skill required assistance to be completed.

Date: /   /   Score:

I Can Brush My Teeth

Skill Progress Log

Attain toothbrush and toothpaste	Y	N
Turn on sink faucet	Y	N
Wet toothbrush	Y	N
Put toothpaste on toothbrush	Y	N
Brush front teeth	Y	N
Brush teeth on right side	Y	N
Brush teeth on left side	Y	N
Brush bottom teeth	Y	N
Brush tongue	Y	N
Rinse toothbrush with water	Y	N
Rinse mouth with water	Y	N
Spit into the sink	Y	N
Turn off sink faucet	Y	N

Directions: Mark Y if the skill is performed without assistance and N if the skill required assistance to be completed.

Date: /   /   Score:

I Can Brush My Teeth

Skill Progress Log

Attain toothbrush and toothpaste	Y	N
Turn on sink faucet	Y	N
Wet toothbrush	Y	N
Put toothpaste on toothbrush	Y	N
Brush front teeth	Y	N
Brush teeth on right side	Y	N
Brush teeth on left side	Y	N
Brush bottom teeth	Y	N
Brush tongue	Y	N
Rinse toothbrush with water	Y	N
Rinse mouth with water	Y	N
Spit into the sink	Y	N
Turn off sink faucet	Y	N

Directions: Mark Y if the skill is performed without assistance and N if the skill required assistance to be completed.

Date: /   /   Score:

I Can Brush My Teeth

Skill Progress Log

Attain toothbrush and toothpaste	Y	N
Turn on sink faucet	Y	N
Wet toothbrush	Y	N
Put toothpaste on toothbrush	Y	N
Brush front teeth	Y	N
Brush teeth on right side	Y	N
Brush teeth on left side	Y	N
Brush bottom teeth	Y	N
Brush tongue	Y	N
Rinse toothbrush with water	Y	N
Rinse mouth with water	Y	N
Spit into the sink	Y	N
Turn off sink faucet	Y	N

Directions: Mark Y if the skill is performed without assistance and N if the skill required assistance to be completed.

Date: /   /   Score:

I Can Brush My Teeth

Skill Progress Log

Attain toothbrush and toothpaste	Y	N
Turn on sink faucet	Y	N
Wet toothbrush	Y	N
Put toothpaste on toothbrush	Y	N
Brush front teeth	Y	N
Brush teeth on right side	Y	N
Brush teeth on left side	Y	N
Brush bottom teeth	Y	N
Brush tongue	Y	N
Rinse toothbrush with water	Y	N
Rinse mouth with water	Y	N
Spit into the sink	Y	N
Turn off sink faucet	Y	N

Directions: Mark Y if the skill is performed without assistance and N if the skill required assistance to be completed.

Date: / /   Score:

I Can Wash My Face

Skill Progress Log

Go to the bathroom	Y	N
Go to the sink	Y	N
Turn on sink faucet	Y	N
Wet hands with water	Y	N
Apply soap to hands	Y	N
Lather soap in hands	Y	N
Rub soap onto face	Y	N
Place hands under running water	Y	N
Gather water in hands	Y	N
Rinse soap off of face	Y	N
Turn off sink faucet	Y	N
Get a towel	Y	N
Dry face off with towel	Y	N

Directions: Mark Y if the skill is performed without assistance and N if the skill required assistance to be completed.

Date: / / Score:

I Can Wash My Face

Skill Progress Log

Go to the bathroom	Y	N
Go to the sink	Y	N
Turn on sink faucet	Y	N
Wet hands with water	Y	N
Apply soap to hands	Y	N
Lather soap in hands	Y	N
Rub soap onto face	Y	N
Place hands under running water	Y	N
Gather water in hands	Y	N
Rinse soap off of face	Y	N
Turn off sink faucet	Y	N
Get a towel	Y	N
Dry face off with towel	Y	N

Directions: Mark Y if the skill is performed without assistance and N if the skill required assistance to be completed.

Date: /   /   Score:

I Can Wash My Face

Skill Progress Log

Go to the bathroom	Y	N
Go to the sink	Y	N
Turn on sink faucet	Y	N
Wet hands with water	Y	N
Apply soap to hands	Y	N
Lather soap in hands	Y	N
Rub soap onto face	Y	N
Place hands under running water	Y	N
Gather water in hands	Y	N
Rinse soap off of face	Y	N
Turn off sink faucet	Y	N
Get a towel	Y	N
Dry face off with towel	Y	N

Directions: Mark Y if the skill is performed without assistance and N if the skill required assistance to be completed.

Date: /   /   Score:

I Can Wash My Face

Skill Progress Log

Go to the bathroom	Y	N
Go to the sink	Y	N
Turn on sink faucet	Y	N
Wet hands with water	Y	N
Apply soap to hands	Y	N
Lather soap in hands	Y	N
Rub soap onto face	Y	N
Place hands under running water	Y	N
Gather water in hands	Y	N
Rinse soap off of face	Y	N
Turn off sink faucet	Y	N
Get a towel	Y	N
Dry face off with towel	Y	N

Directions: Mark Y if the skill is performed without assistance and N if the skill required assistance to be completed.

Date: /   /   Score:

I Can Wash My Face

Skill Progress Log

Go to the bathroom	Y	N
Go to the sink	Y	N
Turn on sink faucet	Y	N
Wet hands with water	Y	N
Apply soap to hands	Y	N
Lather soap in hands	Y	N
Rub soap onto face	Y	N
Place hands under running water	Y	N
Gather water in hands	Y	N
Rinse soap off of face	Y	N
Turn off sink faucet	Y	N
Get a towel	Y	N
Dry face off with towel	Y	N

Directions: Mark Y if the skill is performed without assistance and N if the skill required assistance to be completed.

Date: /   /   Score:

I Can Wash My Face

Skill Progress Log

Go to the bathroom	Y	N
Go to the sink	Y	N
Turn on sink faucet	Y	N
Wet hands with water	Y	N
Apply soap to hands	Y	N
Lather soap in hands	Y	N
Rub soap onto face	Y	N
Place hands under running water	Y	N
Gather water in hands	Y	N
Rinse soap off of face	Y	N
Turn off sink faucet	Y	N
Get a towel	Y	N
Dry face off with towel	Y	N

Directions: Mark Y if the skill is performed without assistance and N if the skill required assistance to be completed.

Date: / /   Score:

www.ingramcontent.com/pod-product-compliance
Lightning Source LLC
Chambersburg PA
CBHW041725070526
44586CB00006B/77